ARCHITECTURE & DESIGN LIBRARY

IRISH COUNTRY

ARCHITECTURE & DESIGN LIBRARY

IRISH COUNTRY

Ann Rooney Heuer

FRIEDMAN/FAIRFAX

PUBLISHERS

A FRIEDMAN/FAIRFAX BOOK

© 1998 by Michael Friedman Publishing Group, Inc.

Library of Congress Cataloging-in-Publication Data available upon request.

ISBN 1-56799-679-5

Editor: Reka Simonsen
Art Director: Jeff Batzli
Layout Design: Jennifer Markson
Photography Editor: Wendy Missan
Production Manager: Camille Lee

Color separations by Colourscan Overseas Co Pte Ltd
Printed in Hong Kong by Midas Printing Limited

3   5   7   9   10   8   6   4   2

For bulk purchases and special sales, please contact:
Friedman/Fairfax Publishers
Attention: Sales Department
15 West 26th Street
New York, New York 10010
212/685-6610   FAX 212/685-1307

Visit our website:
http://www.metrobooks.com

For my loving family circle: Fred, Marlene, Elizabeth, Francis, and Ellen; for Reka Simonsen and Wendy Missan, my two talented editors at Michael Friedman Publishing; and for all the Emerald Isle experts and enthusiasts who have contributed to this colorful portrait of Ireland's country homes—places as warm and enchanting as the Irish themselves.

Contents

INTRODUCTION

Bless the four corners of this house, and be the lintel blest. And bless the hearth, and bless the board, and bless each place of rest.

—William Butler Yeats

Perhaps you've never set foot in an Irish cottage or one of the Emerald Isle's magnificent country manors, but in a stirring way, you've experienced them. Think of the idyllic thatched home in County Mayo in *The Quiet Man* (1952), the Oscar-winning film starring John Wayne and Maureen O'Hara. Or the elegant country estate on Dingle Peninsula in *Far and Away* (1991), which starred Tom Cruise and Nicole Kidman as young Irish immigrants bound for North America. These films spotlight Ireland's legendary "forty shades of green," its vintage homes—rural and regal—and its enduring warmth.

There's no denying that Ireland is renowned worldwide for its lush countryside and hospitality, which draw countless filmmakers and millions of tourists to its shores each year. Yet pastoral beauty is just one of Ireland's many jewels. Its people are another. They've always had a way with words, music, and dance, as well as with beautiful crafts for the home.

In ancient Celtic times, talented artisans were considered *Aes Daána* (the gifted people), and their work was revered. Today's ingenious Irish craftsmen are still cherished for their many contributions to home and church decor, not only in Ireland but around the globe. They're the creators of family heirlooms such as lovely linen tablecloths and napkins bordered with Irish lace, stunning crystal from Waterford, and delicate Belleek china.

In Ireland today, the ancient passion for the land runs deep and you can see evidence of this abiding affection in Irish country—a delightful decorating style that showcases the Emerald Isle's incomparable beauty, creativity, history, and prized natural resources. Irish country is at ease with contrasts, often blending simple, well-worn pine furnishings with more ornate period styles adapted from

OPPOSITE: *With multiple scalloped parapets, grouped chimneys, and arched windows, this Gothic country manor in County Wicklow looks like the setting for a medieval fairy tale. Irish country homes are often surrounded by lovely canals, lakes, or rivers that are made even more beautiful each winter by thousands of visiting swans from Europe and Iceland.*

France, Britain, Italy, and Greece. Ireland's rich yet turbulent history has been colored by centuries of contact with other lands.

From yesterday's seafaring invaders, explorers, and refugees to today's European partners and international investors, countless cultures have landed on Ireland's shores and left their marks on the country's artistry and its architectural landscape. The ancient Vikings are responsible for the touch of Scandinavia that is evident in the designs and hues of many pieces of Irish sculpture and pottery. While Waterford crystal is a hallmark of superior Irish craftsmanship, the country's glassmakers inherited their art from the Normans, who invaded the island in the thirteenth century. And although linen weaving has been an Irish tradition since the Bronze Age, the mechanization of linen and poplin production was introduced by the Huguenots (French Protestants) in the seventeenth century.

Not surprisingly, the British have had a major influence on Irish architecture. They established a strong presence in Ireland with the Anglo-Norman invasion of 1169, and went on to build enormous castles and, later, grand country estates during their nearly eight-hundred-year occupation. The Emerald Isle today is divided into the Republic of Ireland, which is comprised of twenty-six counties no longer under British rule, and Northern Ireland, which encompasses six counties that remain part of the United Kingdom.

Many historians and travel writers believe that some of Britain's finest architectural gifts to Ireland can best be seen in Dublin, the capital of the Republic of Ireland. As the lilting folk song "Cockles

RIGHT: *When the heather is in bloom in Ireland, it's time to pack a picnic basket and escape to the countryside. Wildflowers abound in the spring and summer, and it is not uncommon to see meadows covered with bluebells, wild roses, dog daisies, and buttercups.*

and Mussels" claims, Dublin is indeed a "fair city," graced with an abundance of lovely Georgian homes, terraced houses, and buildings. The Georgian architectural style was fashionable in every corner of Great Britain during and immediately following the reigns of the three King Georges (1714–1820). This style and, later, the Regency and Victorian aesthetics slowly made their way into the Irish countryside and added a classic elegance to many country homes and farmhouses. Also of note are the Dutch-influenced tall red brick homes in such cities as Limerick, and Spanish-inspired architecture in coastal cities such as Galway.

While there are countless country homes in Ireland today, there are a number that stand apart as more formal, grand country manors—"big houses"—that date from the 1700s through the early 1900s. These were built by Anglo-Irish landowners who wanted to live in homes that echoed Britain's fashionable country retreats. The nobility had the means to build such estates, but many transplanted English country gentlemen discovered that the services of eminent European architects were simply out of reach. Instead, these landowners hired local builders and borrowed blueprints from one another to fashion their mansions. In the end, the country homes were

OPPOSITE: *As a mystical land of poets, storytellers, and painters, Ireland celebrates the ancient beauty of its trees and rocks, hedgerows and misty boglands, sea and sky, and the ever-changing quality of its light. Here, two old friends enjoy the blaze of autumn leaves in an arboretum in County Wicklow.*

ABOVE: *This well-preserved stone farmhouse is an architectural antique that not only showcases the skills of Irish builders but the ancient beauty of the island's native granite and limestone. Such stones can also be seen in the more than 3,000 castles and castle ruins that lend haunting grace and beauty to Ireland's countryside.*

ABOVE: *From the library, guests can enter the luxurious drawing room of this lovely country manor, which provides a feast for the eyes from ceiling to floor. The Waterford chandeliers, gilded cornices, and Irish marble fireplace invite admiration, as do the family portraits, landscapes, and nineteenth-century antiques.*

true Irish creations that impressively announced their owners' social standing and reflected such architectural styles and period decor as Georgian, Gothic Revival, Tudor, Victorian, and Edwardian.

While its charming whitewashed walls and golden thatched roof may call to mind an English country cottage, the Irish thatched house has evolved from ancient Celtic days according to its own vernacular traditions. Through the mists of time, building methods and designs were handed down from father to son, and the homes reflected local climactic conditions and available building materials. Most thatched

ABOVE: *The library walls in County Kildare's Leixlip Castle re-create an eighteenth-century print room with decorative French engravings. The ruby-red chairs, lush carpet, and flowering plants all lend bright color to the white room, while the period plasterwork, a mirror from the 1750s, and an unelectrified Venetian chandelier imbue country elegance. Leixlip Castle is home to one of the leading spokesmen for the preservation of Irish country homes, the Honourable Desmond Guinness. He has written that while Ireland's grand homes were fashioned in imported architectural styles, they remain treasures to be proud of, for they were built "with Irish money and Irish skills."*

homes were built from native granite and limestone, cemented with clay or mortar, and plastered and whitewashed with lime inside and out. The design of the traditional thatched home was long, rectangular, and never more than one room deep. Typically, the house included the main kitchen, which had a large hearth, and a bedroom on either side. Centuries ago, thatched homes were sometimes built on a slope to provide an upper living space for the family, with an attached cow byre below.

During Ireland's tragic potato blight and famine (1845–1850) and for several decades afterward, failed farms and evictions caused many laborers to emigrate to other countries. Those who stayed in their beloved homeland had to share their one- or two-room cottages with their cows, chickens, pigs—and often another family. By the 1870s, however, a number of enlarged thatched houses had been built across Ireland to provide rural families with more privacy and space. Some landlords created famine-relief projects that not only enhanced their estates and communities but provided valuable jobs for the Irish.

These days, whitewashed houses are a gentle reminder of Ireland's poignant past, and they are still seen dotting the verdant landscape. Yet vintage homes with a real thatched roof are a rare sight indeed in Ireland. Since the 1800s, it has been acceptable—and a telltale sign of prosperity—to replace thatched roofs with durable Welsh or Irish slate. Fortunately, the Office of Public Works has provided funding for thatched-home maintenance and for the training of a new generation of thatchers to help preserve the character of this charming architectural style.

Since the late 1950s, Ireland has been reinventing itself. Its gradual yet deliberate shift away from an isolated agricultural way of life has created a strong economy empowered by industrial development, foreign trade, and tourism. Because of its recent prosperity, a housing boom across Ireland has spurred the building of new homes, the restoration of the old, and the popularization of Irish country style. You'll find this decorating style in midsize or large Irish homes and farmhouses, in city townhouses where folks long for the bliss of the hearth and the heathered hills, and in small, rural thatched homes and bungalows. Irish country can also be found across the seas, in the homes of the descendants of the millions of Irish immigrants who voyaged to the United States and Canada, Great Britain, Australia, New Zealand, and South Africa in search of employment during the past few centuries.

Perhaps you're like me, and Irish country is a tangible connection to your great-grandparents from County Clare or County Tipperary— people who patiently built furniture, wove baskets, crocheted lace, or pieced together quilts long ago by the light of their turf fires. Maybe you've inherited an antique Irish dresser, a hedgerow chair, Irish lace doilies, or sepia-toned family photos of your kin, and you want to create an authentic setting for such heirlooms in your home. Yet, you don't have to be Irish to appreciate the timeless romance of this decorating style. Its universal language of cheerful colors and floral patterns, simple pine furnishings, more formal European-inspired pieces, delicate lace curtains, and Irish china, crystal, and silver can infuse beauty in any home, anywhere.

OPPOSITE: *Time stands still in the vibrant drawing room of this eighteenth-century Irish manor. The owners have left the walls only partially restored, for effect. A lovely red Oriental rug complements the faded blue walls, and its decorative border echoes the exquisite Georgian moldings.*

CHAPTER ONE

ENCHANTING FACADES
AND ENTRYWAYS

May you have warm words on a cold evening, a full moon on a dark night, and the road downhill all the way to your door.

—an Irish toast

It's said that in Ireland, the land fashions the character of the people. In the same vein, it helps shape and color their country home facades. For example, lively hues and festive folk-art designs can be found in the south, where the weather is temperate and subtropical, while in the cooler, more rugged west and northwest, housing styles and paint preferences tend to be fairly reserved.

In the west and northwest of Ireland, there are the wild Connemara Mountains, the majestic Atlantic coastline, and the hauntingly beautiful Aran Islands. This region is freckled with whitewashed homes, sometimes imaginatively painted with folk-art designs of harps, shamrocks, and flowers, a fairly new trend in facade embellishment seen here and there throughout rural Ireland. In the southwest counties

of Cork and Kerry, where the original *Tir na n'Og* (which means "place of eternal youth") is nestled amid Killarney's romantic lakes and mountains, it has always been a tradition to paint the houses in bold shades. The fashion is now enjoying a renaissance, with many homes wearing such eye-popping hues as black currant purple, post office red, lime green, and tangerine.

The southeast counties are filled with gracious homes and shops often done in demure yellow, pink, or mint green shades—and there is the occasional whitewashed home bejeweled with seashells. Seashell

OPPOSITE: *Imagine living in an ivy-covered castle with its cavernous great halls, chambers, hidden passageways, and perhaps a ghost or two! From about 1790 through the Victorian era, castles were considered the height of Gothic architecture in Ireland. Consequently, many grand and midsize country homes were embellished with romantic turrets, fanlights, and arched windows.*

wall art is a quirky yet delightful Irish vernacular style dating from the 1700s or earlier, and it's most commonly found in maritime areas that possess an abundance of seashells and washed-up shards of colored glass.

Everywhere you travel throughout the Emerald Isle, Irish country homes seem to grow organically out of the purple-heathered countryside. Their facades blend effortlessly with nature, as they are often fashioned from abundant native limestone or granite, as well as brick or wood. In cities and towns, older houses run the gamut from the ivy-covered, boxlike Georgian design with its decorative quoins and graceful proportions to the colorful, gingerbread-trimmed Victorian home with its multicolored or multitextured walls, steeply pitched roof, and

asymmetrical facade. Newer homes are built in a wide variety of styles, often inspired by other traditional European designs. Many of the more traditional homes in Ireland feature a small portico, which is a sheltered entry porch surrounded by columns—a very practical and handy feature for rainy days.

The exterior focal point of the Irish country home is the decorative front door, as proud and sometimes as dazzling as the peacocks found on many grand country estates. The front door expresses the heartfelt Gaelic greeting extended to visitors and family alike, *céad mile fáilte* (a hundred thousand welcomes), as well as the national passion for vibrant hues that are hardly garden variety. For example, the paneled wood doors of Georgian townhouses and homes in Dublin are painted dandelion yellow, magenta, Kerry blue (named after the azure sea of the Ring of Kerry), emerald green, and lavender, to name just a few of the boisterous colors to be seen.

Many farmhouses and old country homes feature polished mahogany front doors, which are left unpainted in order to display the rich grain of the wood. And some of the rural thatched homes still feature the traditional farmhouse half-door, fashioned from wood and painted in vivid colors. Centuries ago, the half-door was inspired by the entrance to the stable of the big house. Practical and sociable, this half-door was bolted to keep curious hens, donkeys, goats, and cattle out and young children inside, while the top half of the door remained open to invite sunshine and visitors to brighten the day.

LEFT: *This engaging hallway holds two striking examples of Ireland's rich heritage of artistry and folklore. The eighteenth-century side table was created at a time when lions, satyrs, or humans were often carved into furniture. The oil painting reflects Ireland's fascination with swans. In the beloved Irish tale, "The Children of Lir," a king's four children were transformed into swans by their heartless stepmother.*

Immediately inside the country home or farmhouse, the warm welcome extended by the gregarious front door continues in the entry hall, a social mecca for hearty hellos and wistful goodbyes. Walls can be painted in such inviting pale shades as lemon, lilac, pink, sky blue, peach, or mint green, or deeper hues such as yellow ocher, pumpkin, light terra-cotta, or dusty rose. Delicate pastel French or Irish floral wallpapers, enhanced by light-colored wainscoting or chair rails, can also be used to keep the mood airy. Whether it's a small space or a long corridor, the entry hall should be treated like a room in its own right, for its ambience makes a lasting impression and offers a sneak preview of the rest of the home's interior. To dress up the entry hall walls, a simple wood-framed mirror or a more ostentatious gilded mirror alongside an arrangement of framed watercolors or prints of Irish landscapes are the perfect choice, evoking a sense of Ireland's great wild beauty.

Proper lighting will add to the radiant welcome of the entry hall, and can be easily achieved with a brass hanging lantern, wall sconces, a delicate Victorian ceiling fixture, or perhaps an antique table lamp that adds a sense of the past. A durable gray or tan flagstone floor resplendent with the patina of age is a hallmark of country home entryways, creating a natural bridge between the rugged outdoor landscape and the cozy interior of the home. The floor can be left bare, or you can enhance it with an Oriental rug or an Irish woolen runner done in a floral, diamond, or curvilinear Celtic design.

Irish country style is easygoing—an eclectic mixture of furniture and accessories. It's perfectly fine to blend the old and the new, the crisply colored and the faded. In the front hall, there's always a place for an antique or reproduction chair, along with a weathered pine pub bench or, better yet, an antique settle bed or an old wooden trunk, perfect for both seating and storage. Other functional and decorative ideas for the entry hall include a colorful umbrella stand, a mirrored hat stand, and a polished antique hardwood or scrubbed pine table to hold hats, gloves, mail, keys, a few family knickknacks, and a vase full of freshly cut garden flowers, so treasured by the Irish.

ABOVE: *Restful green walls accented by fresh flowers, dark mahogany furnishings, and a decorative fireplace surround create an air of understated elegance in this home's entry hall. The textured wool carpet and Oriental rug ground the hall, while a simple display of mementos on the mantel and end table add visual flair.*

ABOVE: *Grazing sheep and cattle are part of the unforgettable pastoral world of this lovely big house in County Roscommon. Of those Irish country mansions that have survived through the ages, a number are privately owned, while others have been transformed into luxurious hotels, schools, convents, and hospitals. Also, some country homes are open to visitors, having been preserved and renovated by the National Trust, the Irish Georgian Society, or Northern Ireland's Ministry of Finance.*

OPPOSITE: *This regal country home in Northern Ireland's County Tyrone was built in the late eighteenth century. It is surrounded by a magnificent estate of bordered and stepped gardens, forests, and lakes. In the spring and early summer, the gardens eclipse the beauty of the home's facade with their sea of azaleas and rhododendrons.*

ABOVE, LEFT: *While the facades of some Neoclassical Irish country homes are restrained in style, a brightly painted front door hints at the spectrum of shades to be found inside the home. Here, a vivid yellow door with a gleaming brass knocker suggests a spirit of warmth and welcome.*

OPPOSITE: *This rustic country home embodies the beauty and strength of the Irish countryside, with its limestone and granite walls, rough pine door, and classic thatched roof. In the past, homes were rethatched regularly to ensure warmth in the winter and cool comfort in the summer. Today, many of these homes have roofs of low-maintenance slate.*

ABOVE, RIGHT: *A back entrance of this old Georgian country home is not only a gathering spot for roosters and hens but the gateway to the home's secret garden—a lovely greenhouse where begonias, lilies, geraniums, and more are grown to fill the house with nature's delicate jewels.*

BELOW: *A traditional Georgian brick quoin design can be seen at the corners of the facade of this gracious home. A faithful friend awaits his family by the lovely front door and welcoming landscape.*

ABOVE: *This daffodil-tinted Georgian home with a stately columned portico is a fine example of the Irish taste for pastel ice cream colors in facade embellishment and interior design.*

ABOVE: *The Italian Renaissance inspired the Georgian style of architecture, which is seen prominently in Dublin and throughout all of Ireland. From the lush grounds, the striking facade of this terra-cotta-hued Georgian home can be viewed. Typical Georgian features include rows of windows with double-hung sashes and many small panes, a gently hipped roof, and a gracious front door with a decorative fanlight overhead.*

ABOVE: *A simple candelabra and an elegant Georgian door with a fanlight are two lovely features of this home's paneled entry hall. The Oriental carpet, family photos, and treasured books provide a welcome that softens the grandeur of the architecture.*

ABOVE: *Stepping into this woodsy entrance hall, visitors are welcomed by the warm glow of the quiltlike tile floor, the grained paneling, and a curious assortment of old Irish walking sticks and knickknacks. The tabletop painting of children under a tree reminds all who enter that summer can't be far away.*

OPPOSITE: *Many of the Neoclassical entrance halls in Georgian country manors have pediments over the doors, pilasters, and high decorated ceilings. This classic entry hall avoids a museumlike ambience through its use of bright colors, a warm Oriental carpet, and a beloved antique Victorian rocking horse.*

ABOVE: *Dressers are prized antiques from yesterday's Irish country kitchen. This early-nineteenth-century dresser is beautiful in the entry hall of a house in County Kildare. Guests can't help but feel welcome here, thanks to the "hen" in the handwoven Irish basket, the "Bahama Coral" walls, and the homey display of colorful plates on the dresser.*

ABOVE: *Illuminated by shafts of sunlight, this Gothic window happily offers a stairway to the heavens for pots of ambitious jasmine, which seem to mirror the outdoor woodlands.*

OPPOSITE: *This home's entry hall displays the owners' passions. The painting on the wall and the antique with the hunting scene attest to a love of nature, while the assortment of crocks and kitchen antiques speak of a reverence for yesterday.*

CHAPTER TWO

FIRELIT SITTING AND DINING ROOMS

To know beauty, one must live with it.

—old Irish proverb

If you've ever stayed in an Emerald Isle home or country inn, you know that the Irish deeply cherish the natural beauty of their island. You can see it in their lyrical paintings, prints, and tapestries, which depict Ireland's lush scenery, flora, and fauna. Man-made beauty is appreciated as well, for many Irish homes are decorated and furnished in Irish-made products, such as paints, wallpapers, woolen carpets, and a wide variety of quality furnishings, fabrics, and accessories.

Carmel Kelly-O'Gorman, an Irish interior decorator and the proprietor of The Lighthouse, a bed-and-breakfast inn located in Kinsale, County Cork, says the decor of Irish country celebrates "the muted colors of spring flowers."

"You see an abundance of floral designs and fresh picked garden blooms in our country sitting rooms and dining rooms," Ms. Kelly-O'Gorman notes, "but rarely do you see accessories that are considered 'stage Irish,' such as china figurines of leprechauns, harps, or shamrocks." Instead, she explains, the Irish surround themselves with fine mementos of their heritage. These can be textiles, such as beautiful handmade laces, linens, and quilts; lovely furnishings crafted from mahogany, walnut, rosewood, and pine; or gleaming silverware, china, and crystal.

In the Victorian era, the Irish sitting room was referred to as the parlor or, in country mansions, as the drawing room. Like the dining room, the sitting room was reserved for the sharing of fine food, drink, and conversation with esteemed guests. Today, this living space is designed for both everyday life and special occasions, achieving its mood of lighthearted ease with a casual blend of floral or geometric patterns,

OPPOSITE: _This treasure of a sitting room reflects Ireland's admiration of British Regency and French Empire decor, as appealing today as it was in the early nineteenth century. An impressive collection of antique Oriental porcelain echoes the Empire emphasis on Chinoiserie and the fact that many Anglo-Irish gentlemen made their fortunes trading in the Far East._

wood tones, and shades of paint ranging in intensity from whisper-soft to boldly vivid. Walls can also be covered in graceful floral print wallpapers accentuated by decorative chair railings or wainscoting. Tall windows are often dressed in floral draperies with brass tiebacks and lace sheers underneath.

For rest and relaxation, a comfy chintz or brocade sofa awaits in the sitting room or library, and its formal lines can be softened with a decorative paisley shawl or an heirloom quilt. Several upholstered fireside chairs, and sometimes a Victorian ottoman and a cushioned window seat, also provide ample places for guests to gather. Pillows on the couch and chairs don't have to match, as a joyful mix of faded plaids, frilly chintzes, checks, and needlepoint add a homey, country feel to the room. Also, small pine or period mahogany or rosewood tables can showcase a wide array of collectibles, such as Irish pottery or small framed photos. Even the table lamps can add to the country decor; popular choices include simple lamps with brass or silver-plated bases and silk Victorian fringed or ruffled shades, Regency stained glass lanterns, or evocative oil lamps or candles, a timeless way to illuminate the home. Floors can be done in soft wall-to-wall floral carpeting, or they can reveal the charming patina of worn wooden flooring, accented by lavish Oriental or Irish wool carpets.

While Irish homes are centrally heated, many rooms are blessed with a fireplace, a romantic focal point where visitors are warmed not only by the wood or turf fire, but by a collection of cherished objects on the mantel. In days gone by, when the kitchen hearth was the center of the Irish home, mantels served as warming shelves and a handy place for pots and seasonings. Today, they're used to display favorite things, and are crafted in a variety of simple or elaborate styles. In many large country homes, decorative fireplaces reflect classic architectural style through intricate stone or wood mantels and surrounds that add a lived-in-for-ages look. Also, many Irish fireplaces are done in beautiful native marble in rich blacks, granite hues, reds, or whites from such places as Connemara and Kilkenny.

Fireplaces in Ireland reflect design styles from a variety of periods and countries. The Georgian style, with its stately overhanging mantel, ornate carvings, and molded step corner on the frieze, is very popular, as is the Regency style, sometimes embellished with French Louis XIV ornamentation or the softer Louis XV Rococo curves and such designs as shells, scrolls, musical instruments, and foliage. The cast-iron or wooden Victorian-style fireplace with raised paneling and a simple semicircular firebox opening is also favored, along with the Adam style, which was created by Scottish architect Robert Adam and his brothers, James and William, who popularized neoclassical themes in housing facades and interiors.

In the Irish country dining room, which is often located adjacent to the sitting room, vintage or reproduction Georgian, Regency, or Victorian furnishings and decorative palettes are often chosen to lend an air of elegant country gentility. Georgian furnishings made of mahogany or walnut typically feature cabriole legs, which curve out at the knee and inward at the ankle to form S-curves. Georgian pieces are also frequently adorned with carvings of lion masks, scrolls, shell ornaments, and mythological forms, as well as hoof-, ball-, or claw-shaped feet. To create an authentic-looking late-Georgian dining room, walls can be painted pea green, turquoise, Chinese yellow, or deep red or pink, or they can be wallpapered to wainscot level in flock (imitation velvet), damask, or silk covered with flora and fauna patterns. Windows should be elegantly dressed with silk or damask draperies gathered into hanging festoons.

Regency-style country dining rooms are generally lighter and brighter than Georgian rooms, benefiting from the delicate beauty of rosewood, satinwood, or mahogany British Regency furniture, with its lion's-paw feet, lion's-head handles, and decorative gilding. Walls can be done in pastel or muted Regency striped wallpaper, or perhaps a salmon pink paint scheme. Windows look appropriately fetching in tied-back silk, linen, or chintz draperies featuring striped or small floral designs.

Also popular for the Irish country dining room are a wide variety of Victorian furnishing styles. If you prefer the deep colors of early Victorian, you can create a dramatic mood in your dining room by blending heavy red damask draperies with dark-hued flora and fauna wallpapers, and adding an abundance of knickknacks, tropical plants, and deep-toned furniture.

The less formal look of the late-nineteenth-century country Victorian style is also popular in the Irish country dining room, for it blends the grace of the Gilded Age with the bright charm of country furnishings, patterns, and colors. You can create this pleasing look with a mahogany, rosewood, walnut, or oak dining table in any shape desired; several Victorian dining chairs; a decorative sideboard or dresser topped with an antique Irish lace or linen runner; and perhaps a matching corner cupboard for china and collectibles. Country Victorian dining room walls are often painted in fresh pinks, roses, mints, and other pastels or are done in light floral wallpapers. Windows are dressed in sheer lace panels or floral chintz, damask, or silk draperies, held in place with elegant tiebacks, tassels, or rosebuds.

Whether you choose to decorate your dining room with period-style furniture or a pleasant variety of simple country pieces, the introduction of lace doilies, jugs, baskets, and stoneware crocks filled with fresh flowers can establish an easy Irish country mood. On the floor, wall-to-wall carpeting or Oriental rugs will provide texture and visual interest, while overhead, romantic lighting can be achieved with a Victorian hanging fixture with a frosted or painted globe, a Tiffany-style stained glass globe, or perhaps a sparkling hand-blown Waterford crystal chandelier.

ABOVE: *A plethora of patterns is a trademark of Irish country decorating. The key to achieving balance is to incorporate prominent areas of complementary solid colors while mixing similarly hued patterns together. Here, the pastel walls, neutral draperies, and white fireplace blend nicely with the muted floral motifs of the brocade sofa, faded chintz pillows, and a graceful Oriental carpet.*

ABOVE: *Because the Irish cherish good company and the art of conversation, their televisions are often banished from the sitting room and the library. This library creates an old-world atmosphere with its carved fireplace surround, ancestral portraits, delicate writing desk, decorative screen, Oriental carpet, and simple yet classic bookshelves.*

OPPOSITE: *Faded carpets and antique furnishings, oft-read books, a blazing fire, and a polished piano create a lived-in, cozy sitting room for family and friends to enjoy sing-alongs and fireside chats. Note how the unembellished window adds to the radiant disposition of the room.*

OPPOSITE: *The striking pumpkin-colored walls reflect the warmth of this drawing room's fireplace. The modern sofa and game table contrast with the simple Irish sugan chair and the stool by the hearth. Over the mantel, the winsome landscape speaks eloquently of Ireland's adoration of horses.*

ABOVE: *Textures infuse country charm in this masculine study. The smooth leather furnishings and soft, geometric-patterned pillows and rug contrast with the rough-grained woodwork of the windows and trunk and the rugged weave of the Irish willow basket.*

LEFT: *The sitting room of this rustic whitewashed home reflects the resourcefulness of the Irish. The cozy fire burns turf dug up from the boglands that cover one-seventh of the island. The chair on the left is made from the timbers of hedgerows that lace the countryside. And the home itself is built from limestone, an amalgam of shells, corals, bones, teeth, and sea lilies that recall the tropical sea that covered Ireland more than 270 million years ago.*

ABOVE: *The warm sherbet walls of this cozy sitting room are the perfect backdrop for an array of chintz-covered chairs, old woolen carpets, casual end tables, knickknacks, sheepskin throws, and a variety of books and games—ideal ingredients for quiet evenings curled up by the fire.*

OPPOSITE: *Antique hardwood furnishings such as this sitting room's decorative writing table can lend authentic period charm to the Irish country home. If you plan to scour antique shops for just the right piece, be aware that the value of well-preserved Irish hardwood furniture is steadily rising. Fortunately, one can still find a good deal of lovely reproduction Irish hardwood furniture currently being made in Ireland and other countries.*

ABOVE: *The nineteenth-century carved fireplace takes center stage in this richly endowed library. An Oriental carpet imparts an air of antiquity, further enhanced by the vases on the mantel and the cabinet's display of first-edition books. Visitors and family can't help but be drawn to this room, as its alluring jewel tones, soft sofas, and fresh flowers create a place fit for the company of great books and sparkling conversation.*

ABOVE: *The stunning gilded mirror over the fireplace adds a sense of spaciousness and light to this picture-perfect library. Here,*
the repetition of delightful blue and yellow fabrics creates an aura of harmony and peace. The floral motifs in the chairs, carpet,
and decorative table complement one another, as do the embellished mirror, bookcases, and intricately paneled doors.

OPPOSITE: *Like a bejeweled crown, the ornate Adam-style fireplace steals the show in this gracious buttery yellow sitting room.*
Note how the bouquets of fresh flowers enliven the old Oriental carpet and how the gold-framed portraits lend an air of country
gentility and ancestral mystery.

OPPOSITE: *This expansive sitting room is a showcase for delicate collectibles from around the world. The homeowners have successfully blended gilded Regency and polished Victorian furnishings and accessories, while quieting the view with a cream sofa and walls.*

ABOVE: *A simple patchwork quilt moonlighting as a tablecloth, a crock of freshly picked blooms, and an array of patterned pillows bring easy, eclectic charm to this lovely Irish drawing room filled with polished antiques and unpretentious upholstered furnishings.*

LEFT, TOP: *Vibrant or richly muted colors are hallmarks of the Irish country home, for warm and cool shades are the perfect antidote to Ireland's mercurial weather. Here, a casual array of floral and geometric patterns in cozy reds complement solid purples, warm wood tones, and lush greenery. The overall effect is a charming country sitting room with a garden disposition.*

LEFT, BOTTOM: *The raw beauty of this library's stone walls, worn pine floors, and venerable church pew creates an idyllic hideaway for reading and day-to-day correspondence. Personal mementos such as framed photos, trophies, and Grandmother's Victorian lampshades imbue charm and a bit of family history.*

OPPOSITE: *The Irish passion for Gothic Revival architecture and furnishings is clearly illustrated in this country home's library. The arches came from a nearby Catholic church, while the ecclesiastical candlesticks, medieval wood carvings, Oriental carpet, and knickknacks have international provenance.*

ABOVE: *Dramatic blue and violet hues in this sitting room are heightened by a background of whitewashed walls and dark, bog oak furnishings. Created from the semifossilized remains of prehistoric forests, bog oak lies beneath the turf in Ireland's boglands. During the Victorian era, the Irish often harvested this wood and transformed it into lovely ebony-hued furnishings, paneling, trinkets, and opulent marquetry tables.*

ABOVE: *This circa-1820s dining hall in a converted granite barn in County Wicklow is the ideal setting for convivial country entertaining. The homeowner designed the chandeliers and added such treasures as the hanging Irish quilt, which is from the 1850s, and the two console tables fashioned from one old pine kitchen table.*

ABOVE: *The two worlds of the Victorian dining room and sitting room dovetail seamlessly in this charming vignette. An abundance of muted floral brocades and velvets fills the rooms, along with highly polished mahogany and rosewood furnishings and a gleaming country floor. The comfortable setting, fresh flowers, and abundant natural light impart the true glory of Irish country entertaining: the communion of kindred spirits amid beautiful, nature-inspired surroundings.*

RIGHT, TOP: *A golden-hued dresser with delicate carvings and glass cabinets is the focal point of this light and airy kitchen. The Irish penchant for fine china and flowers is indulged here, as is the appreciation for classic furnishings, such as the lovely polished table and chairs and the cozy wing chair, designed to offer shelter from drafts.*

RIGHT, BOTTOM: *A long pine table and elegant chairs impart a sense of simplicity to this intriguing Irish country dining room. The high-ceilinged room is done in magnolia and toffee brown faux paneling, enhanced by several works of modern art and a framed display of treasured china. The simple pottery and fresh vegetables on the table and the scalloped chair cushions add to the informal ambience of the room.*

OPPOSITE: *Truly a breathtaking setting, this dining room in a castle in County Offaly often serves fresh fruits, vegetables, and game from its surrounding grounds. The castle was built in the seventeenth century, but was Gothicized two centuries later. Genteel country touches with a semiformal spirit include the scrubbed pine table, wispy curtains, nature-inspired place mats, and charming view of the private gardens.*

ABOVE: *Often, each generation that lives in a big house or castle leaves its own mark by adding fashionable improvements of the day. Ancestral portraits and Neoclassical plasterwork are key focal points of this dining room, as are late-nineteenth-century hardwood furnishings and the Oriental rug that grounds the room's red and gold color scheme.*

CHAPTER THREE
BEGUILING BEDROOMS AND BATHS

D*eep peace of the running waves to you. Deep peace of the flowing air to you. Deep peace of the smiling stars to you. Deep peace of the quiet earth to you.*

—old Gaelic prayer

For two blissful reasons, life in an Irish country home is conducive to tranquil slumber. First, the pastoral world surrounding the home is full of hills and bens (mountains) that need exploring, lakes and streams that invite fishing, and gorgeous gardens that require tending. All that clean, unpolluted Irish air and activity create a sense that all is right with the world, and inspire hearty appetites and deep, restful sleep. Second, when the day is done and the stars come out, the private sanctuaries of the Irish country bedroom and bath await to comfort and soothe with colors, patterns, and textures tenderly drawn from nature.

As you would expect, the bed is the most important feature in country bedrooms large and small. Today, as in the Victorian era, the most commonly seen styles of beds in the Irish country home are either curvaceous and flowing, like climbing vines, or solidly upright and textured, like old cherished trees. Popular styles include vintage Irish brass or cast-iron frames embellished with curlicues or adorned with brass rods, medallions, or knobs. Wood is also a favorite material for beds: note the rustic handmade pine beds and the beautiful, carved four-poster mahogany, walnut, or rosewood beds. Some four-posters have full-testers, or canopies, which can be drawn to keep chilly night drafts at bay. Others beds are half-testers, with romantic canopies of short frilly or lacy curtains.

From the 1700s on, when quilting was a craft born of thrift that was practiced by Irish women everywhere, popular quilt patterns became treasured works of art in the country bedroom. Nowadays, antique quilts are still used as bedcovers, but they also show up as accent pieces on Irish sitting room sofas or kitchen tables. The European duvet comforter, however, is more commonly used for warmth and decorative accent in the bedroom. Duvets are continental quilts that are stuffed with goose or duck down or a synthetic fiber filling. Underneath the duvet, cool muslin, cotton percale, or luxurious linen sheets and pillowcases are comforting choices for bedclothes. Ireland has long

OPPOSITE: *The limewashed walls of this bedroom come to life with a floral stenciled frieze and a dramatic painting of Irish farmers, while the floor and window are warmed by the brocaded draperies and heirloom Oriental rugs. The homeowners wisely decided to leave the fireplace as is, for its centuries-old paint design is still beautiful.*

been renowned for its linens for the home and fashion industry, and today linen duvet covers, sheets, and pillowcases are back in style. People are realizing what their grandparents knew all along—Irish linen is an investment, to be sure, but it offers supreme comfort and long-lasting beauty.

Apart from an attractively dressed bed, there are other furnishings that will enhance the timeless romance of your Irish country bed-room. An old carved or painted pine trunk is the perfect hideaway for extra blankets, sheets, and mementos. For casual seating, a rustic pine bench or velvety ottoman is ideal. A chest or an old washstand can serve as a bedside table and also add storage and display space for family photos, trinkets, and perhaps a small brass lamp. If books are your great escape, create a quiet reading corner by adding an upholstered chair or rocker and a lamp with a fringed or ruffled shade.

ABOVE: *When the Irish consider something to be truly special, they call it "grand." Here, a symphony of warm and cool colors, numerous antiques, and old-fashioned framed prints add timeless warmth and coziness to this grand bedroom. The chintz-covered chaise longue and matching chairs attest to the room's versatility as a place for reading, letter writing, and visiting with family.*

In keeping with the Irish penchant for springtime hues, popular color combinations found in country-style bedrooms include pale pink and green, lemon yellow and pale blue, sea green and ivory, lavender and blue, apricot and ivory, and periwinkle blue and mint green. Color is incorporated into the bedroom not only through painted and gentle limewashed walls, but through a rich array of sprigged, striped, or lavish floral wallpapers. Framed watercolors or botanical prints of cabbage roses, slipper orchids, or pansies bring a touch of the outdoors inside. And in bedrooms with sloping ceilings, the addition of dark stained wooden beams as a decorative element will mirror the look of yesterday's thatched home and farmhouse.

Window dressing is just as important as bed and wall dressing, so consider gauzy lace café curtains or carefree gingham curtains to call to mind the whitewashed home in the country. For a more formal look, tall lace panels or chintz or brocade draperies can complement the color, fabric, and pattern of the bedroom's duvet or quilt. And don't forget to make the most of your bedroom's nooks and crannies. The deeply recessed windows of many farmhouses and thatched homes provide lovely display shelves for terra-cotta pots full of geraniums, an array of baskets, or an assortment of oil lamps or candlesticks. Also, bedroom floorboards can literally be warmed by the addition of Oriental carpets, Irish wool rugs, or handmade hooked rugs that match the color scheme of the room.

For more than a century now, the Irish country bathroom has been a haven for cleanliness, pampering, and comfort. It's a world away from the days of the bedroom chamber pot and the rustic privy at the bottom of the garden. Not surprisingly, since the Victorians believed that "cleanliness is next to godliness," they created many of the designs for the fixtures found in our modern bathrooms, from the bathtub to the pedestal sink. In some older Irish country homes, the bathroom is fairly spacious because it was created from a spare bedroom. But whether it's just big enough for a toilet and sink or large enough for all the amenities your heart desires, the bathroom can be enlivened through the clever use of paint, wallpaper, wainscoting, tile, fabric, and coordinating accessories.

Irish country bathroom floors are done in low-maintenance ceramic tiles, linoleum, vinyl, or rustic, scrubbed pine planks that can be accented with a wash of paint or stenciled designs. Walls can be decorated in a pastel water-resistant paint or in a coated, washable wallpaper in small geometric, ribbon, or floral patterns. Some popular color choices are rose, peach, pale green, light blue, yellow, and ivory. If you prefer a Victorian look, you can blend two colors that are opposites on the color wheel. For example, a deep claret or berry can be contrasted with a pale green, while a bright turquoise looks lovely with a soft yellow. Also, wainscoting painted cream, ivory, or a pale sherbet hue is a wonderful way to invoke a sense of Victoriana.

To infuse a feeling of warmth and romance, the sink basin can be installed in an old pine washstand, table, or converted dresser. If the sink is on a pedestal, you can encircle it with a skirt of colorful pastel chintz, striped, or checkered fabric. Around the sink and bathtub, ceramic tiles can add texture and color. You many want to choose a Victorian-style claw-foot tub or an antique tub encased in wood to add character to the bathroom. Other period items you can use to invoke the Irish country spirit include an antique gilt mirror, a carved pine cupboard, or an old wooden medicine chest surrounded by electrified wall sconces. If you have a large bathroom, a synthetic Victorian-style wicker chair or two (true wicker can't take excess moisture) would be fitting. Frosted or stained glass windows with simple pull-down shades for privacy add an old-fashioned charm. Color-coordinated accessories such as cotton towels, china toothbrush holders, and antique soap dishes with Oriental or floral designs are a perfect touch. Houseplants that thrive in a sunny, humid environment, such as jasmine or scented-leaf geranium, bring a bit of nature indoors, just as the Irish do.

ABOVE: *Season after season, Ireland is known for its lovely gardens and fields of wildflowers. Even on a gray winter day, this eternally blossoming bedroom mirrors nature with its Arts and Crafts wallpaper and a floral quilt. The decor is further enhanced with an intimate blend of mahogany furnishings, a graceful partial bed canopy, the gilded mirror, a Victorian lamp, and a few antique knickknacks.*

ABOVE: *The delicately sprigged duvet on this carved four-poster bed is one of the few modern touches in a room that seems transported from the nineteenth century. The lovely marble fireplace, simple wooden trunk, antique hardwood tables, faded carpet, and treasured paintings together create a warm master bedroom that exudes Irish country spirit.*

LEFT: *Both the brass bed and the iron bed came into fashion in Europe around the 1860s, when metal bedsteads replaced wooden frames with stuffed mattresses, which were a nesting spot for vermin. In Ireland at that time, metal beds and the newly invented coil-spring mattress helped to eradicate bedbugs and fleas, as did the widespread use of factory-made cotton sheets, which could be boiled for cleanliness.*

ABOVE: *Bright red blossoms add a warm glow to this rustic bedroom, highlighted by a one-of-a-kind painted iron bed draped with an antique quilt. The room's refreshing simplicity is enhanced by the woven rush matting, the dappled limewashed walls, and a scrubbed pine chest of drawers.*

ABOVE: *A vision of sumptuous comfort, this bedroom recreates an early-nineteenth-century Regency ambience with its thickly draped salmon-hued walls, its gilded mirror, delicate end table, and antique Chinese prints.*

ABOVE: *To give this country bedroom a French touch, bedcurtains are hung at the head of the bed to emulate a full-tester canopy. The bright chintz fabric echoes the dazzling colors of Irish gardens, as do the fresh blossoms on the windowsill. The limewashed walls and vintage chairs, dresser, and quilt create a romantic country setting that enchants with its intimate tone, rugged and smooth textures, and May Day colors.*

ABOVE: *Endowed with a romantic history of long voyages at sea, this antique leather and brass trunk holds family mementos from several generations. It's the focal point of a restful room that is filled with treasures from near and far, such as the antique Irish lace tablecloth, the imported four-poster bed, and an Oriental carpet.*

RIGHT: *The Gothic-style framework on the picture window of this bedroom suggests days of medieval glory. The rose-colored carpet, lamp shades, and furnishings echo the rich warmth of the wooden ceiling, trunk, and desk, while the big cat trophy skin calls to mind exotic safaris of the Victorian era.*

ABOVE: *Everything's coming up roses in this gardener's haven for slumber. The full-tester bed blends poetically with the delicate wallpaper, while the elegant bedspread, pillows, and lamps prove that white can be a charming contrast to a symphony of colors and patterns.*

ABOVE: *A wee one sleeps in this tiny country bedroom, which is deliciously decorated with lavender paint and a ribbon motif wallpaper. A comfy old pine bed and several cuddly toys, an antique figurine on the windowsill, and a collection of books create a magical place for listening to tales of fairies and giants, kings with secrets, and the enchanted children of Lir.*

LEFT, TOP: *Wallpaper is a magic carpet that can transport a room to long ago and far away. Here, an old-world pattern is cleverly used to make a large bedroom seem more intimate and timeless. Notice how the draperies and bed skirt match the blue and ivory patterned wallpaper, while the ivory quilt and four-poster bed provide dramatic, restful counterpoints.*

LEFT, BOTTOM: *In this restored castle in County Limerick, bedrooms are awash in the sumptuous splendor of the early nineteenth century. Here, a French-inspired canopy with a favorite Napoleonic emblem—the crown— conspire with the brocaded headboard, bed dressing, striped Regency wallpaper, and several delicate portraits to evoke a sense of regal charm and comfort.*

OPPOSITE: *Reminiscent of Josiah Spode's traditional willow-pattern china, the wallpaper, canopy, bedcurtains, and bed skirt of this upscale country retreat are complemented by light and airy Regency-style touches. These include the gilded white end table and the yellow striped scroll-end sofa topped with a frolicking array of floral patterned pillows.*

OPPOSITE: *Pale blue walls and a matching carpet create a soothing background for the heavy, dark furniture and myriad patterns in this elegant bedroom. Touches of white—in the fireplace, framed prints, and on the magnificent bed and chaise longue— brighten the room.*

ABOVE: *An art lover's haven, this eclectic country retreat mesmerizes with its brilliantly patterned bedspread, bold wallpaper, and modern paintings and lithograph on the old-fashioned lacquer and brass bedstead. The crisp white window frame, ceiling, and ivory rug provide counterpoint to the jubilant mix of antiques and patterns.*

LEFT, TOP: *The height of country manor indulgence, this spacious bathroom features a heavenly Gothic window for birdwatching or gazing up at the stars while relaxing in the contemporary bathtub. The Regency wallpaper and coordinating floral curtains and chair make this a room to luxuriate in.*

LEFT, BOTTOM: *Even the bathrooms of many Irish country homes are dressed to impress with a comfortable blend of floral wallpapers, framed prints, antique mirrors, and old-fashioned fixtures. Here, the rolltop bathtub recalls the grandeur of the Victorian era, as do the antique prints of birds, flowers, religious scenes, and the ever-affectionate Cavalier King Charles Spaniel, beloved in Ireland and across the Atlantic.*

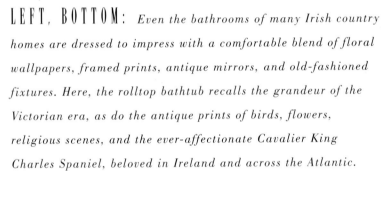

RIGHT: *This bathroom's Victorian ambience comes from a rich mix of garden colors, patterns, textures, and vintage accessories. Opulence is created with the simple chintz swag, the radiant window, and the lush plants and flowers. A touch of lighthearted Irish whimsy is evident in the marble bust masquerading as a hat stand.*

OPPOSITE: *This nineteenth-century copper tub in a Leixlip Castle bathroom has a breathtaking view of a forest of lovely beech trees. In the past few centuries, bathtubs have been fashioned from marble, copper, tin, varnished sheet-iron, and stoneware, as well as the more familiar cast iron, porcelain enamel, and modern-day enameled pressed steel.*

ABOVE: *The walls of this modern country bathroom suggest the decorative ambience of vintage country manor print rooms, where genteel ladies used to display their favorite illustrations. The room's country personality is created by the nature-inspired wall prints, the simple wood plank floor warmed by a neutral rug, and the Irish woven baskets.*

OPPOSITE: *When bathrooms first appeared in Irish country homes in the late nineteenth century, they were symbols of status. Today, reproduction Victorian bathtub enclosures, furnishings, and fixtures are called upon to create period ambience. This room's Victorian sensibility is created with warm wood paneling, the antique chair embellishing the toilet, practical sisal matting, and the country gingham curtains.*

RIGHT: *A passion for antiques is evident in this old-fashioned bathroom, where a charming eighteenth-century-style wash basin and Victorian claw-foot tub provide decorative yet essential amenities. The colorful Oriental carpet, striking red wall, framed prints, and blue and white china ewer also invoke a sense of yesterday.*

CHAPTER FOUR

COZY IRISH KITCHENS

There is no love sincerer than the love of food.

—George Bernard Shaw

Just as there's a lot more to the Emerald Isle's culinary repertoire than brown soda bread and Irish stew, the Irish country kitchen is much more than a room full of state-of-the-art appliances and furnishings. Brenda McTigue, a proprietor of the Clareview House, a bed-and-breakfast farmhouse in Kinvara, County Galway, says that today's Irish country kitchen is truly "the heart of the home"—and it's a grand, affectionate heart at that. The kitchen is where the family gathers to cook, eat, share stories, and read or pursue hobbies, and it's the place where visitors catch up on all the latest news when they drop in for a quick visit or a *cuaird*, a nightly gathering of friends and neighbors. What makes this kitchen so inviting, after all, is its size and cheerful decor, its unbeatable warmth, and its legacy as the center of the home.

Many Irish country kitchens are big enough to accommodate a large family and plenty of friends. There's often room for at least two long pine tables, several rustic benches and Irish sugan chairs, a vintage or reproduction dresser that displays pottery and china, a work area with built-in wooden cupboards, and such modern appliances as a refrigerator, stove, microwave oven, and dishwasher. Often, much of the house is warmed by an immense Aga or Rayburn heat-storage cooker, which sits like a regal throne in the kitchen. Such cast-iron central-heating cookers are a cozy tradition of country life in Ireland. On chilly mornings, the kitchen is especially comforting, for the Aga or Rayburn is always on, operating on solid fuel, gas, oil, kerosene, or off-peak electricity to provide heating and hot water as well as a place to cook and to air laundry. The washing, drying, and ironing of clothes can be done in the kitchen's pantry, which is a casual utility room often decorated in the same colors and patterns of the kitchen.

For long conversations over a pot of tea or something a smidgen stronger, there's also space in the kitchen for a sink-in sofa or fireside chairs upholstered in cheerful plaids or florals. For catnaps, the sofa might be topped with a lovely quilt or a cable-knit throw made in

OPPOSITE: *This Irish country kitchen mixes traditional and modern elements to create a casual haven for memorable family meals. Old-style sugan chairs grace the long farmhouse table, while rough exposed beams partition the ceiling. Contemporary Irish tiles, wooden cabinets, and a gentle Mexican painting set against a vivid yellow wall add a modern flavor.*

County Donegal. Of the countless color combinations you can choose from, Irish country kitchens are often done in white and pale green, cream and rose, beige and peach, blue and ivory (or a more daring blue and sunflower yellow), elegant jet black and white, or vivid red and white. Walls can be painted with an easy-to-clean eggshell finish, limewashed for a dappled, textured look, or papered in tiny floral or geometric prints. Natural or painted wood wainscoting is a practical consideration for this heavily trafficked, utilitarian room. Wainscoting can be installed on the lower portion of the wall, to a height of about three feet (76cm). Overhead, ceilings that feature rough exposed beams lend natural charm and outdoorsy texture to the kitchen, while underfoot, the floor can add a sense of nature through rustic terra-cotta quarry tile, brick, granite, flagstone, or smooth Irish marble tiles. Kitchen floors graced with worn wooden plank floors can be accented with nonskid woven rugs.

Around the sink and counters, Irish or Italian tiles are often called upon for their good looks and quality. Recessed lighting can be cleverly hidden in ceiling beams to provide light over the counters and islands where food is prepared. Above the kitchen table, a lovely Victorian or Edwardian stained glass or frosted globe looks charming, while a casual rattan shade on a hanging light fixture might add a sense of far-away tropical islands—perfect for a sunny yellow kitchen. Windows can be dressed in white or pastel pull-down shades, wooden shutters, or lace café curtains, or they can feature heavier cotton or brocade curtains in geometric or floral prints.

It's fitting to incorporate a sense of the past into the kitchen, for blending the old with the new is a time-honored recipe for Irish country style and character. You may want to include handwoven baskets such as the *ciseog*, a round willow basket for gathering potatoes, or a *creel*, a large willow basket that is carried on a pony's or donkey's back for the hauling of turf or other heavy loads. You can also lend Irish character to your kitchen by using accessories such as an antique butter churn, a wall-mounted wooden plate rack, a vintage wall-mounted saltbox, or iron cooking pots used for creating meals over the turf fire. A St. Brigid's cross, made of straw and hung over the doorway, is perfect—the cross is traditionally dedicated to Ireland's agricultural patroness and asks her for protection from hard times and calamities. A few pieces of rustic handmade furniture are a nice touch, such as a three-legged milking stool, or a brightly painted pine dresser, truly the focal point of the traditional rural kitchen. Vintage dressers have open shelves on top for the display of cups, plates, jugs, and dishes of every size and color. The bottom of the dresser provides storage space for utensils or food, all cleverly hidden away behind closed doors. Very old dressers, on the other hand, were designed with open shelves close to the floor, a perfect nesting place for broody geese or hens. Both the relatively new and the older dressers often feature decorative embellishment such as painted or carved folk-art motifs or classical designs.

While the lovingly-crafted pine and bog oak furniture of Irish thatched homes and farmhouses was designed to last for generations, not all of it has. During the potato famine, some country furniture had to be burned for fuel. Also, when the Irish emigrated, they often could take smaller wooden trunks along with them, but they usually had to abandon their other furnishings. In the past few decades, a good many of the surviving rustic pieces have been purchased by antiques dealers in Britain and the United States. Luckily, there are craftsmen throughout Ireland who are keeping the old craft alive, making excellent reproductions of classic country chairs, beds, tables, and more.

Still being made in the midwest of Ireland is the ash-framed sugan chair, a charmingly simple Irish creation with a replaceable woven seat made of twisted straw or hay rope. Another popular piece is the hedgerow chair, fashioned from the gnarled limbs of common hedgerow timbers and closely resembling North American rustic furniture designs. Also, fine reproductions of the multipurpose pine settle bed can be found. This is a high-sided bench that by day is a

fireside seat with storage and by night can be hinged outward to form a protective bed for children. To protect and accentuate much of the rustic pine country furniture, the Irish would often paint it bright red, blue, or green—or sometimes they would grain their woodwork, coloring it a deep brown to imitate the mahogany or oak found in the big house.

Centuries ago, people would use milk, cow's blood, and animal glue to pigment their paint, but with the advent of modern paints, it has become common for rural folks to repaint their furniture on a regular basis, sometimes creating lively two-tone schemes, such as yellow and green or blue and red, as seen in the country furniture in the south of Ireland. If you're lucky enough to find a vintage dresser or corner cupboard, follow this decorative painting tradition to add immense charm to your Irish country kitchen. For this is a place where the echoes of fiddles playing jigs and reels from yesterday's hearthside *ceilís* can almost be heard, and where today's *cuairds* still celebrate the Irish love of delicious foods, delightful company, and the embracing, enduring warmth of the Irish country home.

ABOVE: *For years and years the multipurpose Aga cooker has radiated cozy comfort throughout country homes in Ireland and the United Kingdom. Above this Aga, the kitchen's canary yellow walls display an eighteenth-century toasting fork and a striking collection of antique blue and white plates and strainers.*

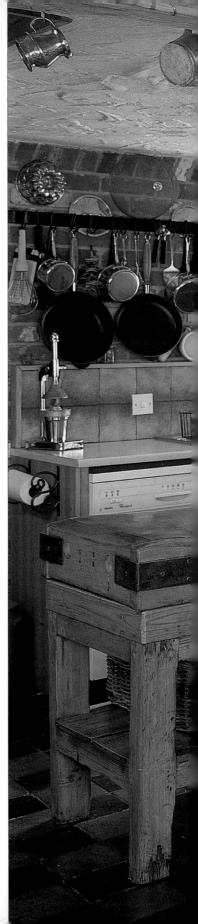

ABOVE: *Whenever high-spirited ceilís were held in yesterday's rustic Irish country kitchen, the limewashed walls of the home would resound with the revelry of fiddles, clinking glasses, and dancing feet. During the festivities, it wasn't unusual for the fiddler to call out, "All around the house and mind the dresser!" Traditionally, the dresser was—and still is—the country kitchen's repository for everyday and fine china, pottery, baskets, oil lanterns, and food.*

RIGHT: *This spacious country kitchen is a chef's dream, for not only is it equipped with a wide array of copper and iron pans, a serviceable butcher-block table, and the latest appliances, it also boasts a charming Irish farmhouse personality. A rustic mood is created through wooden cabinets, exposed ceiling beams, an iron chandelier, an earth-tone tile floor, and country dishes and baskets.*

ABOVE: *Nature's fresh beauty is the focal point in this Irish country kitchen, where floral stenciling on the cupboards, vibrant windowsill plants, fresh garden blooms, and hanging dried flowers create a sense of the outdoors. Generally, the only spot you'll find dried flowers in the Irish country home is in the kitchen, where they're used to create visual interest. Otherwise, fresh flowers are preferred, as dried blossoms are often considered "deceased" in the Emerald Isle.*

A B O V E : *A trompe l'oeil plaque above a kitchen door reminds all who enter that giving joyfully is "doing the will of God from the heart." A lovely pine table set for tea, cushioned sugan chairs, a festively appointed dresser, and an elegant corner cupboard add to the blessings of the room.*

ABOVE: *Two dazzling dressers painted peacock blue add vitality to this simply furnished kitchen. Note how everyday silver, china, spices, and teatime accessories are not only useful but decorative accents on the dressers. A painting of a curious rabbit draws the eyes upward, softening the effect of exposed pipes near the limewashed ceiling.*

ABOVE: *In this well-stocked farmhouse kitchen, many a wholesome meal is prepared amid revered family antiques, such as the hedgerow chair by the fireplace. Because wood was scarce in olden-day Ireland, furniture was often fashioned from hawthorn or blackthorn hedgerow shrubs, or from bog oak that was dug up from its preservative blanket of turf.*

ABOVE: *You can almost smell the fragrant Irish coffee and boxty bread in this spacious country kitchen. The room's warm wooden accents and furnishings, its brick walls and splashes of colorful pottery, and its tiles and porcelain collaborate to create a cozy place for sharing tea and "cut and come again" cake with friends and neighbors.*

RIGHT: *Endowed with two "hearts of the home," this country dwelling features a modern kitchen (glimpsed through the doorway) and a kitchen dating from the 1820s, now used as a sitting room. The handmade hedgerow chairs, pine settle bed, chevvy (spit rack) over the fireplace, assorted lanterns, and unglazed clay floor tiles are cherished reminders of the way Irish kitchens used to look and feel.*

LEFT: *This rustic farmhouse kitchen's fireplace is equipped with an antique Irish cooking crane, which extends over the turf fire for the heating of pans and kettles. Before the twentieth century, the kitchen hearth was the country home's center for cooking, baking bread, ironing, reviving weak newborn lambs and calves, reading, visiting, spinning wool, and weaving unforgettable tales by the firelight.*

ABOVE: *A built-in pine pantry in this large country kitchen provides ample storage space for lovely china, shelves of canned fruits, spices, and herbs, as well as display space for tea canisters. Here, a meal has been prepared and is about to be transferred to the dining room by means of a narrow connecting corridor.*

OPPOSITE: *In the days before electricity, refrigeration, and running water, preparing meals and baking bread over a turf fire was challenging, though deliciously fruitful. Today, the Irish country kitchen pays homage to the old ways by decorating with such kitchen antiques as pine tables, dressers, and stoneware crocks.*

INDEX

PHOTO CREDITS

Elizabeth Whiting Associates: 5, 33, 41, 47, 57, 67, 71, 72 top, 88, 90

Houses & Interiors:
©**Mark Bolton:** 58;
©**Simon Butcher:** 55 top;
©**Michael Harris:** 86-87, 92

The Interior Archive:
©**Tim Beddow:** 2, 20, 32, 77; ©**Simon Brown:** 7, 17,18, 25 both, 28, 34, 38, 39, 43 right, 44, 48, 52, 54, 60, 63, 64-65, 66, 68 left, 68-69, 73, 76 bottom, 91, 94, 95; ©**Schulenburg:** 70, 76 top; ©**C.Simon Sykes:** 74, 89

The Irish Picture Library: 8, 10-11, 12, 13, 14, 15, 21, 22, 23, 24, 26 both, 27, 29, 30, 31, 37, 40, 42-43, 45, 46, 49, 50 both, 51, 53, 55 bottom, 56, 62, 65 right, 72 bottom, 75, 78, 79, 80, 81, 82, 85, 86 left, 93 both